# OYSTERS

# OYSTERS

## By FRED N. GRAYSON

### Illustrated with photographs

JULIAN MESSNER  NEW YORK

Published by Julian Messner, a Division of Simon & Schuster, Inc.
1 West 39 Street, New York, N.Y. 10018. All rights reserved.
A GULF+WESTERN COMPANY

Copyright © 1976 by Fred N. Grayson

Printed in the United States of America

Design by Marjorie Zaum

**Library of Congress Cataloging in Publication Data**

Grayson, Fred N.
    Oysters.

    SUMMARY: Discusses the characteristics, cultivation,
and uses of oysters. Includes material on pearls and
oysters as pets.
    1. Oysters—Juvenile literature. [1. Oysters.
2. Pearls] I. Title.
QL430.7.09G7      594'.11      76-16023
ISBN 0-671-32797-6 lib. bdg.

To Nancy, Scott and Deborah,
but especially to my father,
who instilled in me the love of science
and the quest for the unknown.

Acknowledgment

With special thanks to Fred W. Sieling, Shellfish Consultant, Annapolis, Maryland, and F. William Sieling III, Fisheries Extension Agent, Annapolis, Maryland, for their technical advice and assistance.

# Contents

# 1
# Introducing The Oyster

The eldest Oyster winked his eye,
    And shook his heavy head—
Meaning to say he did not choose
    To leave the oyster-bed

But four young Oysters hurried up,
    All eager for the treat:
Their coats were brushed, their faces washed,
    Their shoes were clean and neat—
And this was odd, because, you know,
    They hadn't any feet.*

Through the years, oysters have been praised in poetry, songs, pictures, and books.

Why oysters? They're not especially attractive. They don't do anything at all. They just sit in one spot—and grow.

But when the oyster has finished growing, it is very valuable. This tiny animal helps support several major industries and feed millions of people.

The sea has given us a magnificent treasure.

*From **The Walrus and the Carpenter,** by Lewis Carroll.

# 2
# The Oyster's Family

The animal we call an "oyster" is called an **ostra** in Spain, a **huitre** (pronounced "wheetr") in France, and **oostritsa** in Russia. In fact, it has a different name in nearly every country in the world. Because of this, scientists have given oysters, and every other living thing on earth, a special name. It is special because it is the same name in every country, and in all languages. Thus, our common edible oyster has the scientific name of **Crassostrea**. When scientists everywhere read or hear this name, they know that it is the common edible oyster. They are members of the oyster family known as **Ostreidae**.

Scientists have also divided all living things into groups that show how all plants and animals are related. The two largest groups are the plant kingdom and the animal kingdom.

The animal kingdom is further divided into **vertebrates** (animals with a backbone), and **invertebrates** (animals with no backbone). Oysters have no backbone, so they are invertebrates.

The invertebrates, in turn, are divided into several related groups. One of these groups includes all the "soft flesh" animals that have no bones. This group is called **Molluska**, which, in English, we shorten

**10**

1.

The popular mollusk family:
1. clam
2. oyster
3. scallop
4. mussel

2.

3.

4.

to "mollusk." Oysters have soft flesh and no bones, and so they are mollusks. The octopus, snail, starfish, clam, mussel, and scallop are all in the same group —they are mollusks, too.

Some of the mollusks grow shells. The oyster grows two shells, and so it is called a **bivalve**. "Bi" means two, and "valve" means shell. Clams, mussels and scallops are also bivalve mollusks. The snail, which has only one shell, is a **univalve**. "Uni" means one.

Scientists believe that oysters began their existence more than 400 million years ago. As the centuries passed, the ocean currents carried baby oysters to places all over the world. In each place, the temperatures were different, the amount of salt in the water changed, and the food supply was different. In order to **survive** (to stay alive), the oysters had to make changes in their bodies. Because of these changes, today there are more than 400 different species of oysters in the world.

Each type of oyster has its own special needs and habits. Some may need more salt in the water than others do. Others may require a greater food supply. Certain oysters may grow faster in warm water, while some may prefer cooler water.

One type of oyster lives on the lower branches and exposed roots of trees in Florida. When these parts of the trees are flooded by high tide, the oysters are underwater. This is the only time they

**12**

1.

These oysters come from various parts of the world. Their differences are caused by their need to adapt to different living conditions: 1. Japanese, or Pacific oyster; 2. European oyster; 3. Eastern oyster, also known as Chesapeake Bay or Virginia oyster; 4. Olympia oyster from the west coast of the United States.

2.

4.

3.

can eat and grow. After the tide has gone down, the oysters are again above water. They stop growing and eating. They must wait for the next high tide.

But most oysters live in water all the time. They can be found in several places: at the bottom of oceans within 100 miles of the coastline, at the mouths of rivers (**estuaries**) which are slightly salty, and occasionally in creeks that are fed by salty tides from the oceans.

# 3
# The Oyster's Shell and Body

Today, most oysters are no larger than about 5 inches. But shells have been found which prove that at one time, oysters were at least one foot long. Except for a few species, oysters grown today would never have a chance to become that large. They are usually gathered before they are six years old, and are still small.

Most bivalves have two equally shaped shells. But the oyster is very different.

The left side, or bottom valve, rests on something solid on the water's bottom. Inside, the bottom valve is hollowed out. This is the part that holds the oyster's body. The right side, or top valve, is connected to the bottom valve by a hinge at the front end. The top shell is thinner and flatter than the bottom one, and is the oyster's roof.

The shell of the oyster contains a chemical compound called **calcite**. The calcite makes the shell hard. The most important chemical found in the calcite is **calcium**. The calcium in the oyster shell is the

The bottom valve of the
oyster is hollow in order
to hold the oyster's body.

The top valve is flatter
than the bottom one, and
serves as a roof for the
oyster.

As the oyster grows older, layers build upon layers, forming a thick, hard shell. This shell is almost two inches thick. Each groove in the shell is the beginning of a growth layer.

same as we have in our bones. It makes the shells hard, just as it makes our bones hard.

The oyster's shell usually grows in the spring and fall. It does not grow in the winter, or in the warm summer months. During its growth period, layer after layer of calcite builds up and ridges are formed. Thus, the shell is thick, rough, and bumpy.

The color of the shell can be different in each type of oyster. The shells may be brown, green, gray, or white, or combinations of these colors.

The valves open and close by the action of a special muscle, the **adductor muscle**. You have many muscles that work the same way. When you make a

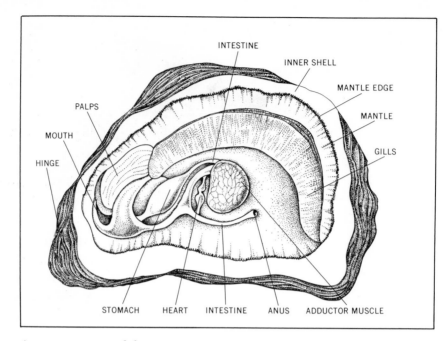

INTESTINE
INNER SHELL
MANTLE EDGE
MANTLE
GILLS
PALPS
MOUTH
HINGE
STOMACH     HEART     INTESTINE     ANUS     ADDUCTOR MUSCLE

A cross-section of the oyster.

fist, you are using the adductor muscles of your fingers to open and close your fist.

An oyster's adductor muscle is very strong. If you've ever tried to open an oyster shell, you know just how powerful this muscle is. A special knife is needed to slip between the two valves, cut the muscle, and pry the shell apart. The muscle is the oyster's protection against its enemies. When there is no enemy around, the muscle relaxes, and the valves open about one-half inch. As long as the valves are open, the oyster can get its food. The oyster's food consists of tiny plants and animals that are floating in the water all around it.

**18**

The body of the oyster is surrounded by a very important, three-layered membrane called the **mantle**. One layer of the mantle makes the oyster's shell. It does this by secreting layer after layer of calcite to form each of the two valves. This part of the mantle also protects the oyster from any un-wanted object that enters the shell. The object might be a grain of sand or a small piece of glass that

The pointer indicates the layers of the mantle. The dark border along the edge of the oyster's body is the cilia.

floats in with the water when the valves are open. By secreting calcite over the object, the mantle keeps it from harming the inside of the oyster.

Another layer of the mantle is sensitive to changes in light or approaching objects. When it is disturbed like this, it will cause the adductor muscle to close the valves for protection.

The third layer of the mantle pumps water in and out of the shell. Under this layer are the **gills** used for breathing and catching food.

The gills are lined with **cilia**, thin little hairs. The cilia move back and forth very quickly, bringing water into the valves. As the water flows over the gills, they strain out oxygen for breathing and food for eating.

The oxygen from the water is absorbed into the blood of the oyster. The blood, which is colorless, is pumped throughout the body by the two-chambered heart. The fresh oxygen in the blood is exchanged for waste products which are taken to the gills and released into the water.

As the food is removed from the water, it is caught on a thin layer of sticky fluid which covers the gills. The gills then move the food to the oyster's mouth. The food that is digestible is pushed into the oyster's mouth by two pairs of muscles called **palps**. One pair of palps lies on each side of the mouth. Food that is indigestible is pushed out of the oyster's valves by the palps. The food that can be digested passes into the stomach.

After the food is digested, what is left is waste. The solid waste material passes through the intestine and reaches the outside through the anus. The liquid waste is removed by the kidneys. The oyster has another way of cleaning itself out. The flow of water through its open valves flushes out solid and liquid wastes.

# 4
# The Birth of an Oyster

The spring and summer is usually the **spawning** season for oysters—their time for giving birth. During this time, the water needs to be warm, in order for the eggs and sperm to survive.

When the adult female oysters spawn, they lay their eggs in the water. Over the next several months, each female oyster can lay almost one hundred million eggs. These eggs are so small that it would take about 600 eggs, side-by-side, to make one inch.

At the same time as the females are laying their eggs, the male oysters release sperm cells into the water. Millions of eggs and sperm cells drift along with the current. When an egg and a sperm join together, the combined cells are now able to grow into another living creature. This is known as **fertilization**.

In less than a day, the fertilized egg becomes a **larva**, or a **veliger**. A larva is the earliest stage of life of many animals and insects. The oyster larva is so tiny, it can only be seen under a microscope. If you were to examine it, you would see that it is shaped like the capital letter "D." Around its edge,

In this photograph, there are two oysters during spawning season. The oyster on the right—the female—is releasing a cloud of eggs into the water. On the left, the male oyster is releasing sperm. When a sperm joins an egg, the egg becomes fertilized.

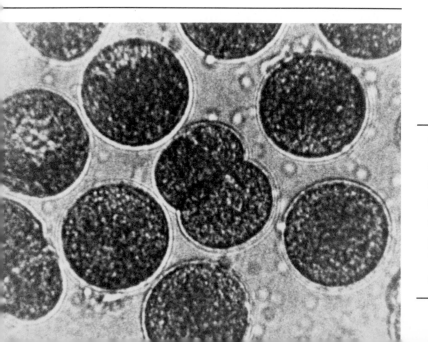

These are oyster eggs, greatly enlarged. The eggs that seem to be splitting—in the center and lower left of the photo—are fertilized. They are in a stage called *first cleavage*.

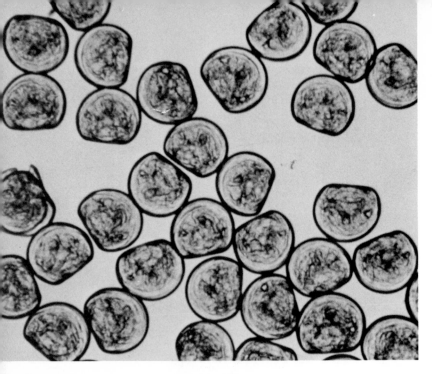

In less than a week after developing, the oyster larva, or veliger, enters a period called the *straight hinge* stage. The long, straight side of the oyster—now shaped like the letter "D"—is the hinge.

you would see a tiny membrane with little hairs on it. This is called the **velum**. The velum is the oyster's swimming organ.

You would also see two tiny valves and a heart pumping blood. The valves are joined together at one side by the strong adductor muscle. Now the oyster larva is beginning to grow larger.

Swimming by means of its velum, it moves back and forth, feeding on **plankton**—tiny animals and plants that float in the water.

The valves grow stronger, and the body is surrounded by the mantle. The larva grows a small foot, which will be used later for moving along the bottom.

**24**

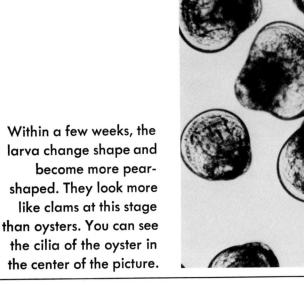

Within a few weeks, the larva change shape and become more pear-shaped. They look more like clams at this stage than oysters. You can see the cilia of the oyster in the center of the picture.

In a few weeks, the shell is hard and shaped something like a pear. The larva is ready to stop swimming. It sinks to the bottom of the water to find a home. Now it is no longer a larva. The oyster has become a **spat**, and it is about 1/16-inch long. With its foot, the spat moves along the bottom, feeling for a place to settle down. If it is too muddy on the bottom, the spat will sink and be unable to breathe or eat. So it looks for something firm on which to settle.

When the spat finds a solid place, it stops and a sticky fluid comes out of the foot. This "glue" sticks the shell to hard material on the bottom. The spat may attach itself to a rock, an old bottle, a sunken ship, or another shell. Hundreds of spat often share the same resting place. This is called an oyster bed.

The spat are now baby oysters. They can no longer move about. Since it does not need its foot and velum for moving, these organs grow smaller, until they disappear.

The oyster takes in food, using its gills and cilia. The young oyster eats and eats, growing larger all the time—unless it is destroyed by its many enemies.

# 5
# Eating, Breathing, Growing

As the oysters begin to grow, there are many things taking place in the water around them that affect their lives.

First of all, the amount of food in the water is important. There must be enough plankton in the water for the oysters to feed on. If there is not enough to eat, they will not be able to grow.

Though plankton is important for the oyster's growth, too much plankton can kill the oysters. Some kinds of plant plankton, such as algae, may grow so fast that it absorbs much of the oxygen from the water. The more algae there is, the more oxygen is removed, making it difficult for the oysters to breathe.

The water temperature also affects the growing process of the oyster. Most species of oysters grow best in temperatures between 55 and 80 degrees Fahrenheit. But they are able to survive in freezing temperature, or in temperatures as high as 100 degrees Fahrenheit. It will take longer for the oyster to become mature if it lives in extremely cold

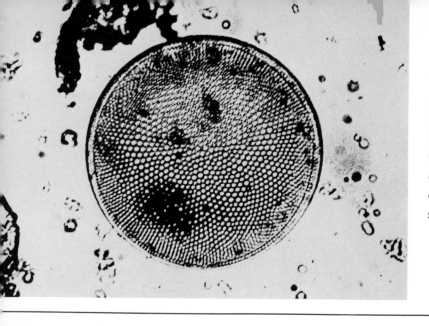

This is a microscopic photo of a diatom, a type of algae. There are hundreds of varieties of these tiny algae, and each looks as if it was created by an artist or sculptor.

temperatures. It will mature quicker in warm water.

The amount of salt in the water also affects the oyster's growth. Too much, or too little salt will kill the oyster.

In pure ocean water, this is not a problem, since the amount of salt does not vary greatly, and oysters like salt water. However, the amount of salt in the water in the estuary of a river can change quickly. The fresh water of the river mixes with the salt water of the ocean, and the change in salt content can endanger the life of the oysters.

Further upriver, there is a smaller amount of salt in the water. The oysters growing there may take an extra year or more to reach maturity, since there is less salt.

Storms cause the death of many oysters living in estuaries of streams. Heavy rains add too

These east coast oysters have grown to different sizes and shapes. Their rate of growth depends a great deal on the temperature of the water. In the warm Pacific water along the coasts of Australia and New Zealand, oysters grow quickly and many develop very large valves. They may reach four inches in size in less than two years. Oysters growing in colder, northern waters may take from six to eight years to develop.

much fresh water, and reduce the amount of salt. The heavy rains and winds also stir up the river bottoms or wash large amounts of mud from the land into the water. The churning sand and mud can cover an oyster bed, smothering the oysters.

It is not easy for an oyster to grow. Any of these things—the amount of food, the saltiness of the water, temperature variations—can affect the oyster's rate of growth, or make the difference between life and death.

# 6
# Enemies

Even if all the other conditions for a long and healthy growth are right, the oyster has dozens of enemies which can end its life at any time.

Human beings are one of the oyster's major enemies. Two hundred years ago, oyster beds were plentiful along the east coast of the United States. But more and more people began eating oysters, and the supply went down. Finally, we learned how to raise oysters, and the oyster supply has increased again.

But water pollution is now the biggest man-made killer of oysters. Until a few years ago, factories and sewage plants dumped their garbage and chemical waste products into rivers. The waste contained poisons which are dangerous to most of the living creatures in and along the water. Plants and animals died. Some chemicals in this waste removed oxygen from the water, so that oysters living in the rivers' estuaries couldn't breathe. They died.

Finally, the government passed laws to control pollution. In many places, dumping chemicals and other sewage into streams and estuaries was stopped. These pollution controls have helped in eliminating the chemical dangers to oysters.

Garbage and chemical waste flow into the water, polluting the streams, rivers, and coastal waters. This garbage may poison the water, which will flow into oyster beds, killing thousands of oysters.

The Red Tide is another threat to oyster beds. It is caused by the fast growth and overpopulation of one particular kind of tiny plankton. It grows so fast and becomes so plentiful that the water looks red.

Along the coasts, thousands of fish die from Red Tide. Oysters may survive this disease, but if people eat the contaminated oysters, they will become ill. The Red Tide occurs in tropical ocean water, and can occur almost anytime. In the mid-Atlantic states, from Georgia to Rhode Island, there is something similar to Red Tide, but the microorganisms are not poisonous to people. Fortunately, scientists are usually able to spot an outbreak of these diseases, and prevent the contaminated oysters from reaching the public.

The oyster has other dangerous enemies. Some plants, like eel grass, may cover the oyster beds and smother the young mollusks.

But the greatest menace to oysters are starfish. When starfish discover an oyster bed, they arrive in large schools and kill thousands of the oysters.

**32**

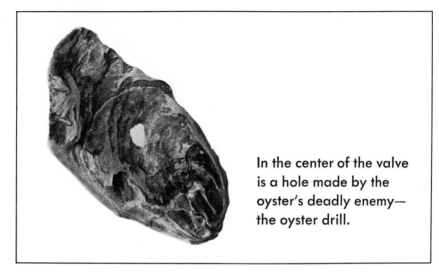

In the center of the valve is a hole made by the oyster's deadly enemy—the oyster drill.

To protect the oysters, oystermen lower large bundles of cotton rope to the oyster beds. The starfish become entangled in the cotton. They are brought up, and then are dropped into large pots of boiling water where they are killed.

The oyster drill (a type of snail) is another deadly enemy. It crawls on the oyster's shell, and with its sharp tongue, drills and saws through the thick shell. When it has finished drilling, the oyster drill dines on the unprotected oyster.

There are also pea crabs which may crawl into an oyster shell. They make their home there, eating the oyster's food, depriving it of nourishment. If large numbers of these crabs invade the oyster, it will die.

The boring sponge bores tiny holes through the oyster shell, and leaves it looking like a bee's honeycomb. Sea otters also feast on oysters. The otter picks the oyster from its bed, cracks open the shell with a rock, and eats the oyster.

There are also dozens of different fish that feed on the oysters. They have strong jaws and crushing teeth that can grind up the oyster's shell, to get at the meat.

And if all these enemies aren't enough, there are still diseases that may infect the oysters and destroy complete beds. Three of these diseases are the most common killers. Humans are not affected by them, and it is rare that we would ever eat an oyster that has one of these diseases.

Illnesses in oysters also occur in waters with high salt content, and when the temperature is hot. If oysters are transferred from their beds into water with less salt, before the summer, they may escape these illnesses.

Scientists are continuously working to develop cures for oyster diseases. They also strive to develop new strains of oysters that are resistant to diseases.

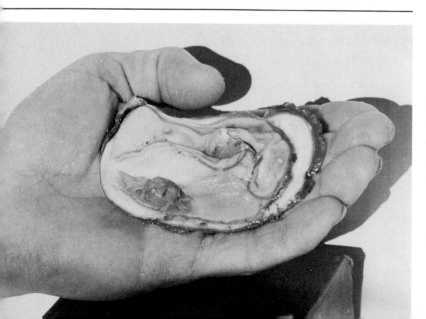

In the lower left side of this oyster is a pea crab which often lives inside the oyster's shell. Pea crabs can do great harm to an oyster by depriving it of food and by irritating its tissues.

# 7
# Oyster Farming for Food and Byproducts

Billions of oysters do survive and grow to maturity, only to find themselves gathered by oyster farmers for food.

We know that primitive people ate oysters. Historians found that in the beginning of the first century, the Romans developed a taste for oysters. They ate so many that they were forced to import them from England. But most of the oysters shipped from England died on the long voyage to Rome, since there was no way to keep them fresh. Finally a Roman, Sergius Orata, found that by planting baby oysters along the shore line, he could control their food supply. He was able to develop healthy, large, and tasty oysters. He was probably the first oyster farmer.

Today, oyster farming is an important industry. The United States and Japan are the largest commercial growers of oysters in the world. Private oyster farmers own undersea land, or, in the United States, they often lease areas from state governments. These areas are marked with stakes or floating buoys, and they are the oysterman's "farm." The individual states also operate their own farms.

The farmer buys spat from suppliers, who have raised them. The spat, which are usually attached to old oyster shells known as **cultch**, are planted on the farmer's oyster beds. The best time for "planting" is in the warm weather of June, July and August. These spat are known as **seed oysters**.

Though not as efficient as dredges, there are still a few oyster "tongers" around today. Note the long poles which are the handles of the rake used to gather up oysters.

When the seed oysters are about one year old, the farmers gather them up. Years ago, they used tongs, scissor-like rakes that gathered only small amounts of oysters at a time. Today, most oyster-men use dredges to scoop up large loads of oysters from the bottom. Dredges are boats with large me-chanical rakes on them.

The year-old oysters may then be sold to

**36**

Commercial oyster growers use these mechanical dredges to harvest their crop for market or for resale to other growers. In this photo, the dredge is draining and cleaning off a basket of freshly picked oysters.

other oystermen who move the oysters to their own beds in deeper water. They are left to develop for three to six years.

To cut out much of the handling of the growing oysters, new methods have been developed for raising oysters. Hatcheries have been built to grow oysters in special tanks. There the water is controlled for temperature, amount of salt, and the right kind

The growth rate of young oysters can be increased in special tanks. The youngsters will get enough food, salinity, and correct water temperature.

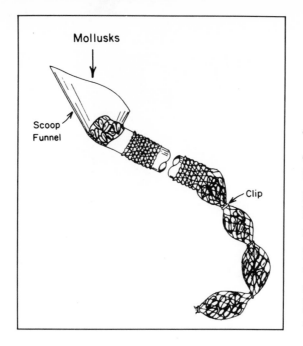

Mollusks

Scoop
Funnel

Clip

This drawing shows one of several ways of farming oysters. Oysters are poured through a funnel into a plastic netting. The net is clipped at various points to separate the oysters into specific quantities. They may be kept in this netting until they are harvested.

of food. This process also shortens the length of time it takes for an oyster to reach maturity.

Another time-saving growing method has been discovered. The seed oysters are kept in long, plastic net bags. They can be moved from bed to bed, without ever being taken from these bags. At maturity, the oysters can be sold, still in the plastic bag in which they grew.

Like any crop, oysters must be harvested when they are ready for market. Again, the dredges gather in the oysters, which are then sold to food companies. These mature oysters are known as **market oysters**. They are also sold to seafood stores, or to restaurants that sell them **on-the-half-shell**.

The shell is opened with a special knife, and the raw oyster is served on the open shell. The meat

**38**

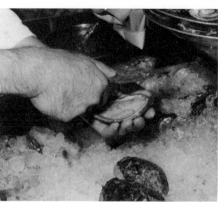

a. Opening an oyster is an art. First, a special, flat-bladed knife is inserted between the valves.

b. e.

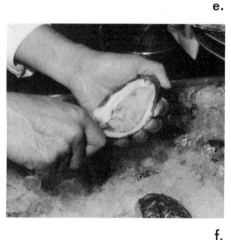

b. The adductor muscle attached to the top valve is cut, releasing the oyster.

c. The valves are pried open, and the hinge broken to separate them completely.

d. The top valve is removed and discarded.

c. f.

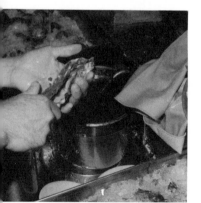

e. The knife is inserted under the oyster, and the other side of the adductor muscle is cut.

f. The fresh, raw oysters are left in half their shell (valve), and served on ice, to keep them cool and tasty.

is plump and light gray. It is usually eaten with lemon juice squeezed on it, and then dipped into a spicy mixture of ketchup, horseradish, and hot tobasco sauce.

There's an old saying, "Raw oysters should only be eaten in those months that have the letter 'R' in it."

There are two reasons for this belief. The months without the letter "R" are May, June, July and August—the warm summer months. Years ago, before people knew about refrigeration, oysters would spoil during the warm weather. Today, of course, we can keep the oysters cool and protected so they will not spoil. Now, oysters are sold all year around.

Actually, the worst month for eating raw oysters is September, when they are tired from spawning. Their meat is not so tasty as oysters served during other months.

The oyster meat is washed, packaged, and sold to stores and restaurants. You can buy frozen, breaded, or canned oysters in most grocery stores and, in their shells in a fish store. Or, you can order them in a restaurant. They can be served fried, boiled, roasted, or baked. Oyster stew is a very popular and delicious soup. Very often oysters are used in the stuffing that fills your Thanksgiving turkey.

Throughout the years, we have become more concerned with the importance of eating a balanced diet to maintain good health. Oysters contain most of the important vitamins and minerals that we need for healthy growth. An average serving of six oysters will supply more than the recommended daily allowance (RDA) of iron and copper, and a large amount of the required protein, iodine, calcium, magnesium, vitamin A, and other important minerals. Few foods are better balanced nutritionally than oysters.

Shuckers remove the oyster meat from the valves. The meat is packaged and sold. The shells (valves) are sold to other oyster growers, feed and fertilizer manufacturers, and construction industries.

None of the oyster goes to waste. Those oysters not eaten raw are sent to **shucking** houses where the shuckers remove the shells. They are sold back to oyster farmers who use them as cultch for the bottom of the oyster beds.

The shells are also used for their lime content.

Scientists have found that by grinding the oyster shells and combining them with chicken feed, the chicken's eggshells become stronger. This means there will be fewer broken eggs when the farmer ships them to market.

Lime is also extracted by burning the oyster shells in furnaces. The ash that remains is the lime. This lime is used in making steel and in plaster wallboard for use in houses.

About one percent of all fertilizers (plant food) containing lime comes from oyster shells. Lime from oyster shells is especially good for crops such as clover, soybeans, and peas.

Oyster shells are sold to road builders who use them like gravel. Many roads paved with oyster or other seashells, such as some roads in eastern Texas, are called "shell roads."

# 8
# Pearls From Oysters

Have you ever seen a pearl? They come in many sizes, shapes, and colors. They're used for necklaces, pins, earrings, rings—all kinds of jewelry.

Pearls are valuable because of the beauty of their iridescence.

To understand **iridescence**, put a few drops of oil into a dish of water. Then take the dish outside into the sunshine. You will see colors that shine and sparkle on top of the water. The sun's light bounces back from the oily surface and is bent. When light is bent, it breaks into different colors. That coloring is iridescence. It is the same sparkle you see on the surface of pearls. Regardless of the pearl's color, it will still have this iridescence.

Where do pearls come from? From inside an oyster. Oysters make pearls to protect themselves. It sounds strange, but it's true.

Suppose you were eating a walnut, and a piece of shell stuck against the side of your mouth. Before it began to bother you too much, you would cough or spit it out, or scrape it out with your fingers. But if something small and irritating gets into the oyster's shell, there is no way for the oyster

**Pearls are used for rings, pins, and earrings.**

to remove it. It might be a piece of shell or a grain of sand, or anything small enough to float into the oyster when the valves are open. To protect itself against the irritation of this piece of foreign matter, the mantle of the oyster gives off a fluid called **nacre**.

The nacre comes from the outer edge of the mantle, and flows over the irritation inside the oyster shell. The nacre begins to cover the little object. Once it starts covering, it doesn't stop. It coats the little irritant and covers the inside of its shell. Layers of nacre begin to build up. By some unknown process, the little nacre-covered objects in certain oysters become perfectly round, while others are not so regularly shaped. These nacre-covered objects are pearls.

An oyster cannot begin to produce nacre until it is about one year old. And then it takes 3 to 6

**44**

Shown here is the inside of an oyster shell found in China. These tiny statues of Buddha were inserted in the oysters and left for several months. When they were removed, the statues were covered with nacre.

years to make an average size pearl about the size of a pencil eraser.

Though all mollusks secrete a substance like nacre to form a protective covering, only the oyster can make a true pearl. Other mollusks produce only a chalk-like piece without the true pearl's iridescence.

If you were to cut a pearl in half, you would find the little piece that started it all, at the very center of the pearl. You could probably try to make a pearl yourself. But you would quickly learn how difficult it would be, and how truly amazing the oyster is to be able to do it.

If it were possible to make a fake pearl, you could start with a small piece of mollusk shell or a tiny pebble. This would be the core of the pearl. Then you would cover the piece with a smooth, shiny liquid which will dry and harden. Nail polish is suitable and easy to work with. Cover the piece again and again until it is 100 times bigger than the piece you started with. Do you think you could do this within a year? How much nail polish do you suppose it would take? Would you be able to make it perfectly round?

Once you began this experiment, you would quickly realize that you can't make a pearl this way. Only the oyster can make a pearl. So in order to produce enough pearls to sell throughout the world, growing and harvesting of pearl oysters has become a big industry.

# 9
# Growing and Harvesting Pearls

For hundreds of years, divers have been searching the ocean's bottom for pearl oyster beds. The oysters were gathered, placed in baskets, and lifted to the surface. Other workers opened the oysters and removed the pearls. These are called **natural pearls**.

But over the years, so many pearl oyster beds were used up that today there are very few left. Because these are so hard to find, their pearls have become very expensive.

However, scientists have discovered a way to make oysters produce pearls. These pearls are called **cultured pearls**.

Cultured pearls are produced by oysters grown on underwater farms. Most of these farms are found in Japan, Australia, Burma, Okinawa (an island that belongs to Japan), and other areas of the Indian and Pacific oceans.

The Chinese were the first people to uncover the oyster's secret of pearl production, back in the 13th century.

Scientists and naturalists continued to study the oyster. In the 19th century, the Japanese began to understand the secrets of making pearls. They inserted various irritants into the shell, but most of the oysters died or failed to produce a pearl. Finally, in 1893, they harvested their first cultured pearls. The pearls were badly shaped, but it was a beginning. After many years of research, they perfected their techniques so that pearl oyster farming has become an important industry.

Japanese oyster farmers lower flat bamboo rafts covered with seed oysters to the bottom of the water. In other countries, the seed oysters are kept in baskets.

Once the seed oysters have been set in place, they begin to grow. They are left alone until they are a year old and about one inch in diameter. Then the rafts or baskets are raised, and the oysters are

An aerial view of a Japanese oyster farm, showing the bamboo rafts from which are hung the baskets of growing oysters.

moved from their beds into deeper water. They are left to mature for two more years.

Because pearls will only form in water that is more than 55 degrees Fahrenheit, the oysters sometimes have to be moved to warmer waters. This explains why the cultured pearl industry remains in the warmer countries.

In their third summer, the oysters are collected and sorted. The smaller oysters are put back in the beds to continue growing. Those that are too old, unhealthy, or dead are thrown away. The oysters that have been selected to make pearls are brought to a laboratory for a special operation.

A little irritant around which the oyster will build its pearl, is **implanted** (put inside the oyster

In Japan, the *Ama* women used to dive for natural pearl oysters. Today, they do not look for oysters, but tend the oyster farms. They look for stray oysters and lost baskets, remove starfish, and sort the oysters. Their face masks enable them to see clearly under water. Their unusual clothing was designed to protect them from scrapes on the rocky bottom.

These are the floating worksheds of a Japanese oyster farm. Supplies are kept aboard these rafts for the workers. On the left are the baskets used by the Ama women to collect stray oysters.

shell). This little object is usually a tiny polished piece of shell from a mussel, another type of mollusk.

The piece of mussel shell is covered with some mantle tissue from another oyster, and then implanted inside the oyster's body. The implant is called a **pearl-sac**. Then the oysters are placed into beds again, in warm water. The nacre begins to cover the pearl-sac. After a few weeks, when the oysters have recovered, they are moved to deeper water. To make sure they stay healthy, they are raised to the surface from time to time, to be inspected and cleaned.

Finally, they are moved to slightly cooler water to finish growing. The cooler water temperature makes the nacre thin and very reflective, giving the pearl its iridescence.

Three to five years later, the pearl oysters are harvested for the last time. By now, more than

**50**

Pieces are being cut from an oyster's mantle to be used in the implant for other oysters.

A skilled technician performs the delicate operation of inserting the pearl-sac into an oyster.

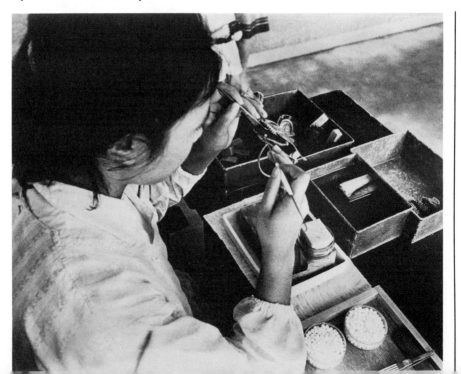

This oyster has produced a beautiful, round, cultured pearl from an implant.

half have developed pearls, but only a small number of them are of the highest quality. The pearls may be white, pink, cream, blue, black, gray, or a combination of these colors.

Not all of the pearls are round. Some have an irregular shape and are called **baroque**. Others have grown against the inside of the shell and must be scraped off. These are **Mobe** pearls. They are used for pins and earings that need a flat side in order for them to be mounted.

The pearls are sorted according to size, shape, luster (shine), color, and texture. Pearls may be very tiny or between 6 and 10 millimeters round—about ½ an inch. Some pearls grown in the South Pacific may be much larger.

An irregular Mobe pearl
is used in this handsome
pin.

These highly trained
pearl sorters in Japan
must have at least seven
years of training for this
specialized job.

One of these two necklaces is strung with equal-sized pearls; the other is strung with pearls of increasing size.

The task of sorting pearls is difficult, since no two pearls are exactly alike. To make one necklace, about 10,000 pearls must be carefully sorted to find enough pearls similar in size, shape, and color. When the pearls are selected, a hole is drilled in them, and they are strung. These strings of pearls are sold at auctions to pearl dealers. The dealers buy them in large quantities, and sell them to jewelers throughout the world, to be made into necklaces and other jewelry.

The inside of the pearl oyster shell can also be used for jewelry and decoration. These shells are often lined with a thin layer of nacre called **mother-of-pearl**. It is as beautiful as the pearl itself. Before the development of plastics, sections of the shells were cut out to use for buttons. But now plastic buttons are much cheaper to make. So most of the mother-of-pearl is used for jewelry and for decoration on furniture, carvings, combs, brushes, boxes—all kinds of things.

**54**

# 10
# Oysters in Your Home

If you live along the Pacific or Atlantic coasts, or in any area where oysters live, you may find old oyster shells in the sand.

As you feel the thickened shell, think about all the years that the oyster was growing. Is the inside still shiny with mother-of-pearl? If it is, take the shell home and cover the inside with clear nail polish. The polish will prevent the iridescence from fading.

Break the shell apart with a hammer or a rock. You might then be able to peel away some thin layers of mother-of-pearl. Examine it more closely under a magnifying glass.

With a little luck, you might be able to find a live oyster. Or if there is a shucking house in your neighborhood, perhaps they will give you live oysters. Your local fish store might sell oysters. If you can get them, why not try raising oysters at home or in school?

To grow oysters you will need the following supplies:

Fresh oysters from the sea.

Five-gallon fish tank
Packaged sea salt for five gallons of water
Eight pounds of limestone or calcite chips
Two oysters
Assorted shells and rocks

Begin by washing out your tank with clear water from the faucet. **Do not use any soap or detergent**. When the tank is clean, place it in the spot where it is to remain. If you try to move the tank after it is filled with water, it will be too heavy to lift.

Now, follow the directions carefully on the salt package. It will tell you exactly how much water is to be mixed with the salt. Pour the salt into the tank, and add the water. Stir the salt around so that it dissolves. The water will look cloudy.

The chips for the bottom of the tank must be washed carefully. They are usually covered with a fine dust, and if they are not cleaned, the dust will remain in the tank. It will darken the water and

**56**

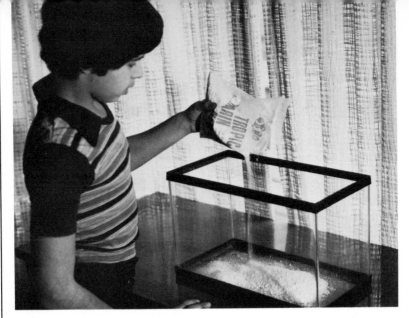

Sea salt comes in
premeasured packages.
Make sure you follow the
mixing directions
carefully, so there is the
right amount of salt in the
water.

Use a large spoon or your
hand to stir the salt
water. Stirring will help
dissolve the salt faster.

form a dirty film on the surface. The best thing to do is put the chips into a large strainer, and mix them around as the water flows through them. Again, do not use soap or detergent.

When the chips are clean, add them to the tank. Move the chips around with your hands so they are higher at the back of the tank than the front. This is to make them look more interesting. Then add shells, rocks, or pieces of colored coral for decoration.

Some salt-water fish are able to live with oysters. Perhaps your pet store owner can recommend them to you.

As for plants, it is better not to put them into the tank, even though they look pretty. Plants stop the growth of algae on which the oysters feed. A light over the tank, kept on for about eight hours, will help the algae to grow along the sides of the tank. When the algae sticks to the glass, you should scrape it off and let it drift in the water. This frees the algae so that it can float, which will help the oyster to feed.

Before you add the final touch—the oysters— the tank must sit for two or three days so the salt will dissolve completely. Also, the temperature of the water will become room temperature, best for growing oysters.

Once the oysters are put in the tank, you will have to be patient. It may take a few days for them to become accustomed to their new home. But then, they will begin to feed.

**58**

Here is the finished oyster tank, with two oysters and several decorative shells. Above the tank is a small light to help the algae grow. The salt has dissolved and the water is clear.

Having finally grown accustomed to its new home, this oyster is just beginning to open its valves.

You will see their valves open wide, and the water flowing through them. Occasionally, the oysters will snap their shells closed to flush out waste. If you tap on the glass, they will also close their shells.

If the oysters are cared for, they will continue to grow in your tank for two or three years. This would prove that you have managed to make an **environment** for the oyster. It means that your tank contains everything necessary to keep the animal alive and well, even though the oyster is not in its natural home on the bottom of the ocean.

# Glossary

ADDUCTOR MUSCLE      A muscle that pulls one part of the body to another.

BAROQUE      Irregular shaped pearls.

BIVALVE      A mollusk that has two shells hinged together.

CALCITE      A common mineral found in limestone, marble, chalk, and oyster shells.

CALCIUM      A metal that is a chemical part of Calcite. It gives strength to the oyster's shell.

CILIA      Thin, short hairs attached to the oyster's gills. They are used to bring water into the valves.

CRASSOSTREA      Scientific name of the common oyster. It is, commercially, the most important oyster.

CULTCH     Stones, bottles or old shells that make up the bottom of the oyster bed, to which the baby oysters attach themselves.

CULTURED PEARLS     Scientifically developed pearls, grown within cultivated oysters.

ENVIRONMENT     All the surrounding conditions that affect or influence living and development.

ESTUARY     The part of a river where it meets the ocean's tide. Its mouth.

FERTILIZATION     The joining of male and female cells (sperm and egg) to create another living being.

GILLS     Organs used to obtain oxygen and food from the water.

IMPLANT     The placing of the pearl-sac into the oyster.

INVERTEBRATES     A group of animals without a backbone.

IRIDESCENCE     Rainbow-like colors that give pearls their beauty.

LARVA (veliger)     The young, invertebrate animal. The veliger is the larva form of mollusk.

MANTLE     A three-layered membrane that covers the oyster's body. It makes the oyster shell, creates pearls, opens and closes the shell, and pumps water through the valves.

MARKET OYSTERS     Mature oysters ready for distribution to food companies.

MOBE     Pearls grown on the inside of the oyster's shell. Also known as Blister Pearls.

MOLLUSKA (Mollusk)     Any invertebrate with a soft, fleshy body and a shell that partially encloses the animal.

MOTHER-OF-PEARL     The lustrous nacre that coats the inside of the pearl oyster's shell.

**NACRE**     The lustrous secretion from the mantle of the oyster. The flow is stimulated by any object entering the oyster's shell. It forms pearls and mother-of-pearl.

**NATURAL PEARLS**     Pearls that have grown inside oysters, found in natural oyster beds.

**ON-THE-HALF-SHELL**     Raw oysters served on one valve, topped with spicy condiments.

**OSTREIDAE**     The oyster family, made up of three members: Crassostrea (the common, commercial oyster); Ostrea (small, cold water oysters); and Pycnodonte (large, heavy shells.)

**PALPS**     Muscles used for pushing food into the oyster's mouth.

**PEARL-SAC**     Implant in the oyster composed of mantle tissue and a piece of shell, around which the nacre will flow to create a pearl.

**PLANKTON**     Floating, microscopic plants and animals.

**SEED OYSTERS**     Very young oysters used for cultivating and implanting.

**SHUCKING**     The process of removing the shells from the oysters. Both the oyster's meat and shells are sold and used.

**SPAT**     Young oysters, after larva stage.

**SPAWNING**     The time when fish, mollusks and other sea animals lay eggs and sperm into the water in order to give birth.

**SURVIVE**     To remain alive throughout a period of time.

**UNIVALVE**     A mollusk that has one shell or valve.

**VELIGER**     See larva.

**VELUM**     A thin, cilia-covered membrane used to move the oyster veliger through the water.

**VERTEBRATES**     A group of animals with backbones.

# INDEX